The Doge's Palace
in Venice

Cover
Paolo Veronese, *Juno Offering
the Ducal Crown to Venice.*
Sala del Consiglio dei Dieci.

Facade of the Doge's Palace
facing the Piazzetta.

Translation
Richard Sadleir

Eugenia Bianchi
Nadia Righi
Maria Cristina Terzaghi

The Doge's Palace in Venice

Electa

The Doge's Palace

The earliest permanent settlements in the lagoon of Venice seem to date back to the period following the fall of the Western Roman Empire (476), caused by the inroads of barbarian peoples. These early settlements were gradually consolidated until they were seen as outposts of the Byzantine Empire.

In the 7th century, the first Dux or, in Venetian dialect, Doge was installed, probably with the approval of the Eastern Emperor, who made the local administration autonomous. This role, suspended at various times due to rivalry between various families, became permanent in the mid-8th century on the election of Doge Teodato Ipato.

By the start of the 9th century, Venice was increasingly independent, isolated by its distance from the capital and confirmed by a religious difference: the dedication of the city to St. Theodore, the patron saint of Byzantium, was replaced by the cult of the Apostle Mark, whose remains, according to later historians, were supposedly preserved in the city.

In 810 Doge Angelo Partecipazio moved the seat of government from Malamocco to Rivoalto, and sought a suitable location for the organs of government of the new state. A site on land belonging to him on the islands of Rivoalto was chosen and at building commenced on the *palatium ducis*. This is still the site of the Doge's Palace, though nothing remains of the 9th-century structure. We know nothing about the form of the original palace; but we do know that in the 13th century it had a main block that was purely defensive in purpose, laid out on a square ground plan, a sort of mediaeval castle. Of the older structure, some parts of the four corner towers remain.

In the 10th century the palace was partially destroyed by fire during a revolt against the Doge Pietro Candiano IV. Its reconstruction, under Doge Sebastiano Ziani (1172-1178), eschewed defence in favour of a typically Venetian-Byzantine style. The palace was thus adapted to the contemporary changes in the city's institutions and the creation of new officers of state, who shared power with the Doge. Hence the need for greater space and more chambers than before. An 18th-century print shows us how the Doge's Palace was originally structured.

Along the side on Piazzetta San Marco there was the building known as *ad jus reddendum* (the Law Courts), with a colonnade on the ground floor and a loggia opening on the first storey; the offices were on the upper floor. The side facing the quay had the *palatium commune* for deliberative assemblies: this was made by

Statue of Eve on one of the corners of the Doge's Palace.

Doge's Palace, facade on the quay.

adapting the outer wall of the old building to serve as an inner wall, and then building on one side out towards the Piazzetta and on the other towards the tower on the corner of the Ponte della Paglia. Few traces remain of this phase of construction: all one can see is a base in Istrian stone and some brick paving laid in a herringbone pattern.

Further extensions became necessary in the late 13th century. In 1297 the *Serrata* of the Maggior Consiglio considerably increased membership of the legislative assembly from 400 to 1,200. Because of the need to enlarge the council chamber, it was decided to take in the adjoining rooms rather than build a new one on the upper storey. Work began in about 1340 under Doge Bartolomeo Gradenigo (1339–1343) and was completed in 1362, despite delays caused by the plague of 1348. For this phase of the work we have the names of some of the craftsmen: in 1361, for instance, documents mention a certain Filippo Calendario, stonemason, and Pietro Basejo, *magister prothus*, who must have been assisted by numerous other masons and sculptors, given the rapidity with which work progressed.

The extensions also affected other parts of the building and when they were finally complete the palace must have looked much as we see it today.

In 1424, under Doge Francesco Foscari (1423–1457), it was decided to rebuild what remained of the palace of Doge Ziani facing onto Piazzetta San Marco, both to improve its stability and for aesthetic reasons. The new building was designed as a continuation of the Doge's Palace. It starts from the relief of *Justice*, level with the thirteenth column of the loggia, and unites the end of the Sala del Maggior Consiglio with the main entrance to the palace, flanked by the two original structures. This new building—none of the names of the workmen are recorded—has a colonnade on the ground level and loggia above, both in the outer elevation and the elevation on the courtyard.

On the same floor as the Sala del Maggior Consiglio there is a huge chamber, known as the Sala della Libreria (later the Sala dello Scrutinio). The windows and pinnacles of the gable repeat the decorative motifs on the sea facade. The elevation facing Piazzetta San Marco was completed with the construction of the Porta della Carta (1438–1442) by Giovanni and Bartolomeo Bon.

It was later decided to rebuild the part of the palace to which access was provided by this new door. The construction of the lobby, known as the *androne Foscari*, took some years, as is shown by the presence of the arms of Doge

Anonymous, Perspective plan of the city of Venice, 15th century.

Cristoforo Moro (1462–1471); work was completed under Doge Giovanni Mocenigo (1478–1485).

In 1483 a serious fire damaged much of the palace and once more extensive reconstruction was necessary. A building arose on the same site, joining the Ponte di Canonica with the Ponte di Paglia: this work was entrusted to Antonio Rizzo, who also designed and constructed the staircase opposite the Arco Foscari.

By 1497 work had progressed as far as the second arch after the staircase, and was completed as far as the Doge's apartments in 1501 when Agostino Barbarigo died, after taking possession of the new building. Meanwhile Antonio Rizzo had fled from Venice after being accused of embezzlement. The work was then turned over to "maestro Pietro Lombardo," who was commissioned to oversee the completion of the sculptural decoration of the facade and the Scala dei Giganti.

In the following years setbacks to the Venetian state slowed work, so that when Antonio Abbondi lo Scarpagnino took over from Pietro Lombardo, little progress had been made. In 1531 it was finally decided to rebuild the old part of the palace; and ten years later a passage was built to link the Doge's apartment with the Sala del Maggior Consiglio. The arms of Doge Francesco Donà, elected in 1545, mark the completion of the marble façade on the ground and upper storeys. In the years that followed, the old wooden staircase that linked the buildings on the canal was replaced and work was only completed in 1559, under the supervision of Pietro Piccolo.

Finally the palace was complete, and each administrative organ had its own chambers. The installation on the staircase of the two great statues of *Mars* and *Neptune* by Sansovino in 1565 can be said to have marked the end of this important phase of work.

Courtyard of the Doge's Palace, 18th-century print.

In 1574 another fire destroyed part of the chambers on the second floor. Particularly badly damaged were the Sala delle Quattro Porte, the ante-chamber to the Collegio, the Collegio itself and the Senate, but fortunately without harming the main structure. The panelling, and above all the decorations, were immediately repaired. But as soon as work was complete in 1577 another devastating fire damaged the Sala dello Scrutinio and Sala del Maggior Consiglio, completely destroying the paintings by Bellini, Pordenone and Titian that had decorated them.

There were various plans for refurbishing the wing; finally it was decided to accept a proposal by Giovanni Antonio Rusconi, who set to work to restore its original appearance. The work was rapidly completed between 1579 and 1580, under Doge Nicolò da Ponte. Until then the palace had contained not only the Doge's residence, government chambers and law courts, but also housed the prisons (on the ground floor to right and left of the Porta del Frumento).

It was only in the late-16th century that Antonio da Ponte ordered the construction of the Prigioni Nuove, designed by Antonio Contin. They were completed by around 1600 and linked by the Bridge of Sighs. The transfer of the prisons to the new buildings vacated space on the ground floor of the palace. Restructuring by Monopola at the start of the 17th century completely altered the ground floor with the creation of a colonnade like that on the Renaissance facade. At this time the Scala Foscari was also pulled down and replaced by the present internal staircase; and in the empty space between the facade of the Arco Foscari in the courtyard and the corner of the palace, Monopola built a facade with an arcade on the ground and upper storeys, terminating in the structure containing the clock (1615).

The functions of the Doge's Palace changed at the end of the 18th century, when the Austrian domination replaced the French. In 1807 it became the Court of Appeal; in 1812 the Marcian Library was moved to the Sala del Maggior Consiglio and later to the Doge's Apartments. The library was soon joined by the Archaeological Museum.

In the 1860s restoration work done, but it was only in 1908 that the library was moved to its

present premises, and in 1918 the Archaeological Museum was also transferred. In 1924 the Italian state, owner of the palace, turned the building over to the municipality, and it was opened to the public as a museum.

The oldest part of the Doge's Palace is now the **facade** facing the quay, with its 13th-century sculptures at the corners of the building. They are attributed to Filippo Calendario or certain Lombard artists, like the Raverti or Bregno families. On the side facing the Ponte della Paglia they represent *Tobias and the Angel Raphael* (above) and the *Drunkenness of Noah*; towards Piazzetta San Marco are the *Archangel Michael* (above) and *Adam and Eve*. Both on this side of the palace and the side facing the Piazzetta there used to be a number of 14th-century capitals, replaced by copies in the 19th century and now in the Museo dell'Opera. The central balcony dates from the 15th century: it was dated (1400–1404) by Pier Paolo Dalle Masegne

Doge's Palace, facade facing the Piazzetta.

"Filippo Calendario," Aristotele Dialecticus *on the capital of the Sapienti.*

*View of the Doge's
Palace.*

*Detail of the statue
of Eve at a corner
of the Doge's Palace.*

*Doge's Palace seen from
the Ponte della Paglia.*

*Doge's Palace, the
openwork of the loggia.*

and harmonises well with the 14th-century architecture of the facade. The coping of the balcony was refashioned in 1579, when the statue of *Justice* by Alessandro Vittoria was added to replace the original, by an earthquake in 1511. The statue of *St. George* is an 18th-century work by Giovanni Battista Pellegrini. The other statues represent *St. Theodore*, the *Cardinal Virtues*, *St. Mark*, *St. Peter* and *St. Paul*. On the facade facing Piazzetta San Marco, near the thirteenth column, a bas-relief of *Justice Enthroned* has been inserted among the pierced *tondi* of the loggia. The balcony at the centre of the side on the Piazzetta was built in the early 16th century in imitation of the balcony facing the quay. The sculptural treatment of the corner towards the Porta della Carta is extremely effective, representing the *Judgment of Solomon* and, above, the *Archangel Gabriel*: critics now attribute these works to Bartolomeo Bon. It is likely that the overall scheme embodied in the various groups of sculpture is meant to express the principal features of Venetian society, while suggesting parallels between the Doge's Palace and the Palace of Solomon and also representing it as the seat of Justice.

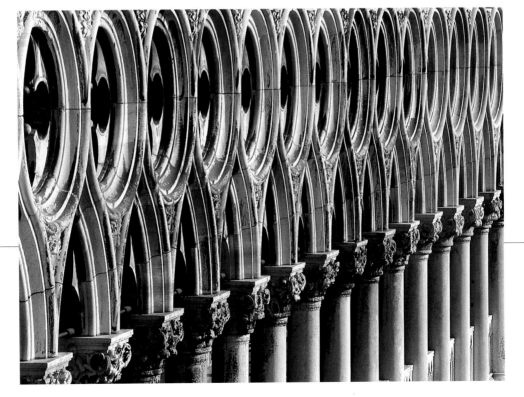

Work began on the **Porta della Carta**, the monumental entrance to the palace, in 1438 and continued for the next four years. On the architrave is carved OPUS BARTHOLOMEI. The name of this entrance seems to be due to the fact that public scribes would gather here, or perhaps public records ("cartarum") were stored nearby.

In Decorated Gothic style, it is remarkable for its rich sculptures and ornate surfaces, which were originally painted or gilded. It is flanked by two pinnacles within which are two figures of *Cardinal Virtues*, attributed to Bregno, and above is the bust of *St. Mark the Evangelist*, surmounted by the figure of *Justice* bearing its iconographic attributes of a sword and scales.

Above the cornice over the door is Francesco Foscari—under whose dogeship the work was carried out—kneeling before the lion of St. Mark. This is a work by Luigi Ferrari and was commissioned to replace the original destroyed in 1797.

Admission to the Doge's Palace today is by the Porta del Frumento, on the side facing the quay.

The Porta della Carta.

The Porta della Carta, detail with Doge Francesco Foscari kneeling in front of the lion of St. Mark.

Following page, above *Filippo Calendario, capital.*

Following page, below *View of the room in the Museo dell'Opera of the Doge's Palace.*

The **Museo dell'Opera** contains thirteen capitals from the palace's outer loggia: they were replaced with copies during restoration work in 1876–1887. Twelve of them, with anthropomorphic decorations and some with Latin inscriptions, date from the phase of work that began in 1340 and scholars now generally attribute them to Filippo Calendario; one is early 15th-century work.

Among the capitals from the loggia there is a very fine one with the *Creation of Adam and Eve, The Planets and their Houses*. The rooms in the museum also have twenty-nine capitals from the loggia, all dating from c. 1340–1450, notable for their highly decorative qualities and lack of inscriptions.

The two facades of the east wing of the palace, which look onto the courtyard and canal, were both built at about the same time, and can be dated with some precision by the arms of the doges reigning during the various phases of work.

The facade onto the canal goes back to the dogeship of Giovanni Mocenigo (1478–1485), whose arms appear on the pilaster at the entrance to the Doge's chamber. The facade looking onto the courtyard is slightly later, as shown by the arms of Doge Marco Bar-

barigo (1485–1486) on the first capital on the corner of the Cortile dei Senatori. Under his successor, Agostino Barbarigo (1486–1501) work proceeded steadily on both facades and reached the seventh arch of the arcade after the Scala dei Giganti, up to the piano nobile.

Meanwhile work continued on the interior, and must have been well-advanced by 1498, the year when Rizzo fled. In 1514 it had already reached the eleventh arch, while the arms of

Francesco Donà (1545–1553) placed a little further on seem to suggest that work had slowed down on the courtyard front, while the arms of Leonardo Loredan (1501–1521) on the canal facade indicate that work had made more progress on that side. In the courtyard there are also the *well-heads* bearing the signatures of the craftsmen who cast them, Nicolò de Conti and Albergeto.

On the south side, running the whole length of the courtyard, is the Renaissance facade built after the fire of 1483 and completed in the mid-16th century. Access to the upper storeys of the Doge's Palace is by the **Scala dei Censori**, on which work began in 1525 to replace the previous unroofed outdoor staircase; it leads from the ground floor to the second *piano nobile*; it was probably designed by Scarpagnino.

On the upper storey is the loggia, which is distinguished by the *Bocche di Leone* inserted in the walls and the plaque of Alessandro Vittoria, commemorating the visit of King Henri III of France.

The **Bocche di Leone** on the walls of various parts of the Doge's Palace, in particular the loggia, Sala della Bussola and Sala della Quarantia Criminal, served for delivering anonymous accusations. They had the form of a lion's head—hence their name—and the open mouth was the slit for letters. Each Magistracy had its own Bocche di Leone.

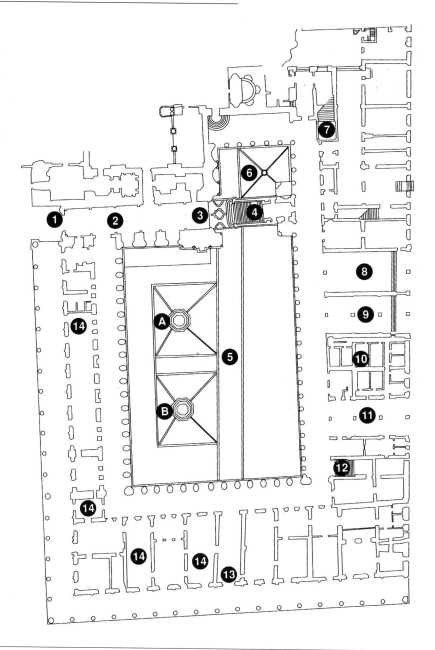

Scala d'Oro
and the Doge's Apartment

The gap between the Doge's residence and the Palazzo di Giustizia was filled by constructing the **Scala d'Oro**, designed by Jacopo Sansovino in 1538, after the most famous architects of the day—Palladio, Sammicheli, Rusconi—had been approached with the commission. It was completed in 1559 by Scarpagnino under Doge Lorenzo Priuli, whose arms appear on the inner side of the archway. The arms on the outer side are of Doge Andrea Gritti, under whom work began. The structure consists of various flights of steps leading to the Doge's Apartments on the first floor on the canal side, and then to the second floor, where there are the great assembly chambers and those used for the high offices of the Venetian state. At the sides of the doorway are two statues, *Hercules Killing the Hydra* and *Atlantis*, by Tiziano Aspetti. Ascending the **Scala d'Oro**, on the first floor we come to the **Doge's Apartment** (see the plan on page 82), completely rebuilt after the fire of 1483 to designs by Antonio Rizzo and Pietro Solari, called Lombardo, under the Doges Giovanni Mocenigo and Marco and Agostino Barbarigo, on whose death some details were still incomplete. However, the suite must have been in use by 1492.

The chambers are largely devoid of furniture because furnishings were regarded as the doge's private property and hence on election each doge brought his own and his heirs removed them at his death. At the centre of the

suite is a large central chamber running the whole length of the palace and set at right angles to another long chamber with three smaller rooms on either side.

The Scala d'Oro.

Sala degli Scarlatti

The first chamber as one enters from the Scala d'Oro is the **Sala degli Scarlatti**, once used as an ante-chamber for the doge's councillors. Of the ancient interior there still remains the carved ceiling, designed and probably executed by Biagio and Pietro da Faenza. Between the two windows is the chimney-piece, the work of Antonio and Tullio Lombardo, dating from c. 1507: its classical decoration is typical of the taste of the period.

The two marble reliefs above the doors depict *Doge Loredan Before the Virgin* and the *Virgin and Child*. The various rooms of the Doge's Apartment are hung with paintings, some of which come from other rooms in the palace, while others are of unknown provenance.

In the Sala degli Scarlatti are works like Giuseppe Salviati's *Resurrection* and Titian's *Madonna with Child and Angels*, whose dimensions suggest it must originally have adorned the landing of the staircase that leads from the Cortile dei Senatori to the first-floor loggia.

Sala delle Mappe, Sala Grimani and Sala Erizzo

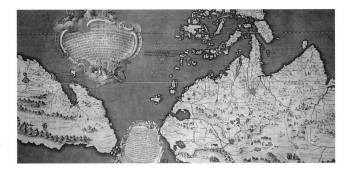

The **Sala delle Mappe** (or **Sala dello Scudo**) is decorated with a series of maps painted on canvas in the Cinquecento, but restored in the 18th century. The **Sala Grimani**, named after Doge Marino Grimani (1595–1606), whose arms are at the centre of the ceiling, is decorated with a frieze painted with a series of allegorical figures, including *Venice* and *St. Mark*.

The splendid carved ceiling ane fireplace are original, by Lombardo, while the stucco embrasure was added under the Doge Pasquale Cicogna (1585–1595), whose arms it bears. On the walls are three paintings of the *Lion of St. Mark*, one by Jacobello del Fiore (signed and dated 1415), one by Donato Veneziano (1459) and one by Vittore Carpaccio (signed and dated 1516). The next room is the **Sala Erizzo**, decorated with a frieze with *putti* and symbols of war. On the walls are paintings, including the *Presentation at the Temple*, *Noah's Arc* and the *Ascent to Calvary* attributed by the critics to Gerolamo Bassano.

From the Sala degli Stucchi to the Sala degli Scudieri

The **Sala degli Stucchi** (or **Priuli**) was originally laid out for Doge Lorenzo Priuli (1556–1559) and subsequently refurbished in the 18th century by Doge Lorenzo Grimani (1741–1752), who added, among other things, the stucco decorations of walls and ceiling. It is adorned by various paintings, including a *Portrait of Henri III* attributed to Tintoretto, a *Holy Family*, an *Ascent to Calvary*, a *Noli Me Tangere*, a *Circumcision* and *Christ Praying in the Garden of Gethsemene* by Giuseppe Salviati, and an *Adoration of the Shepherds* by L. Bassano.

The **Sala dei Filosofi**, which serves as a passageway, has an 18th century stucco ceiling and is decorated with twelve canvases with portraits of philosophers painted in the 18th century and originally intended for the Biblioteca Marciana.

From this room a small staircase joins the Doge's Apartments with the chapel above. Over the staircase door is a *St. Christopher* by Titian (c. 1523). The **chapel**, at present closed to the public, was designed by Scamozzi in 1593. On the altar is a statue of the *Madonna and Child* by Jacopo Sansovino. The walls are decorated with *trompe l'œil* architecture and the ceiling with allegorical ornaments.

On the walls of the **Sala Corner** there are paintings related to the history of the Corner family. The next room contains the *Dead Christ* by Giovanni Bellini. The **Sala degli Scudieri**, originally an antechamber, has been stripped of its original decoration and now contains two paintings by Domenico Tintoretto.

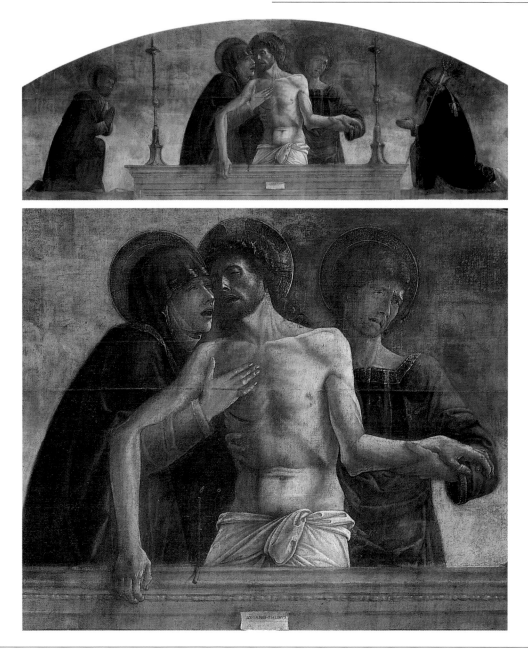

Giovanni Bellini,
Dead Christ, *full view*
and detail, signed
JOHANES BELLINUS.

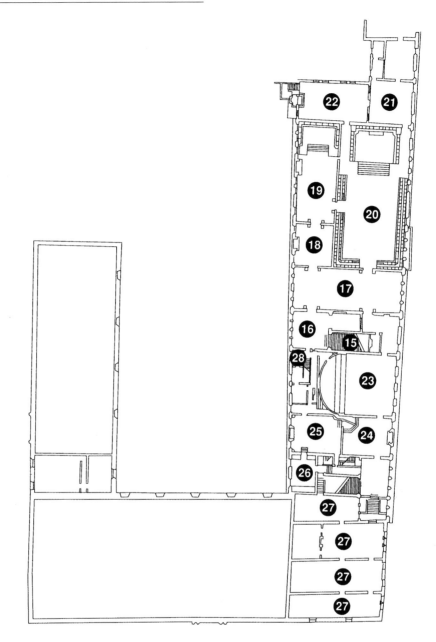

Plan of the second floor

15. Scala d'Oro
16. Atrio Quadrato
17. Sala delle Quattro Porte
18. Sala dell'Anticollegio
19. Sala del Collegio
20. Sala del Senato
21. Antichiesetta
22. Chiesetta.
23. Sala del Consiglio
dei Dieci
24. Sala della Bussola
25. Sala dei Tre Capi
26. Sala degli Inquisitori
27. Armoury
28. Passage to the Piombi

Atrio Quadrato

Continuing up the Scala d'Oro
to the second floor, we reach
the **Atrio Quadrato**.
This is a fairly small chamber
that serves as a hallway to the
great state-rooms. The
decorative scheme was
completed in the mid-16th
century under Doge Gerolamo
Priuli (1559–1567), whose
portrait on the ceiling was
painted by Jacopo Tintoretto
(1564–1565). The portrait is
flanked by biblical scenes and
putti, by artists of the school
of Tintoretto. During the
dogeship of Priuli, the walls
were adorned with four
canvases by Tintoretto,
now in the Sala del
Anticollegio. In their place
are other 16th-century works:
*St. John Writing the Book
of Revelations* and the
*Annunciation to the
Shepherds*, ascribed by
scholars to Paolo Veronese
and Gerolamo Bassano;
the *Expulsion of Adam
and Eve from Eden*,
attributed doubtfully
to Paolo Veronese or Paolo
Fiammingo, and *Christ
Praying in the Garden
of Gethsemane* of the school
of Veronese.

*Paolo Veronese
(attributed to)*, St. John
Writing the Book of
Revelations. *Atrio
Quadrato.*

Sala delle Quattro Porte

The next room is the **Sala delle Quattro Porte**, clearly having the function of an anteroom, giving access to other chambers. It runs the whole depth of the palace and was formerly the venue for meetings of the College, and hence of the *fanti* (or ushers). Its present arrangement, with the four doors which give it its name, columns standing out from the walls, the statues above and the mullioned windows opening onto both Rio di Canonica and the inner courtyard, is the result of its restructuring in 1483. The décor was altered at various times and finally completely renewed after the fire of 1574. The commission for the new design was given to Andrea Palladio and Giovanni Rusconi, and the work was executed by Antonio da Ponte. The barrel-vaulted ceiling is decorated with white stucco and gilding, in harmony with the refined taste of the age, and is ascribed to Bombarda (1575–1577). The frescoes on the ceiling are by Tintoretto, painted between 1578 and 1581 and based on a scheme devised by Francesco Sansovino. The frescoes in the circular panels in the ceiling represent *Juno Offering Venice the Peacock and Thunderbolt* and

Venice Breaking the Chains of Captivity; the one in the centre represents *Venice Symbolically Receiving Dominion Over the Adriatic from Jove*; while the eight ovals depict the cities and regions of the mainland (*Verona, Istria, Brescia, Padua, Friuli, Treviso, Vicenza, Altino*). The ovals of the lunettes represent *Philosophers*. The four portals, designed by Palladio, are surmounted by groups of sculpture alluding to the chamber into which they lead. The wall decoration, perhaps

begun by Titian in the mid-16th century, was completed later (1595–1600) under Doge Marco Grimani. The canvases represent *Doge Antonio Grimani Kneeling before Religion* and *St. Mark* (begun by Titian and completed by his nephew Marco Vecellio); the *Venetians under Gattamelata Defeat the Visconti and Retake Verona* (by Giovanni Contarini); the *Legates of Nuremberg Receive the Laws of Venice from Doge Loredan* (by Carlo and Gabriele Caliari); *Henri III Arrives at Venice, Welcomed by the Doge*

and Patriarch (by Andrea Vicentino); *Doge Pasquale Cicogna Gives Audience to the Persian Ambassadors* (by C. and G. Caliari); above the windows onto the courtyard, *Venice Rising Above the World* (by Nicolò Bambini). Over the windows looking onto the canal is a work by Giambattista Tiepolo, *Neptune Offering Venice the Riches of the Sea* (1740), which replaced a painting by Tintoretto of *Venice Wed by Neptune Who Makes Her Queen of the Seas* that was damaged.

Sala del Anticollegio

The **Sala del Anticollegio** formed an anteroom for ambassadors and delegations waiting to be received by the Venetian state. The original decorative scheme, destroyed in the fire of 1574, was similar to that of the previous chamber.

The room was restored first by Palladio and then Scamozzi. The central fresco, *Venice Conferring Rewards and Honours,* is by Paolo Veronese. On the wall with the windows there is a chimney-piece in Palladian style, with statues by Scamozzi while the upper relief by Tiziano Aspetti. The walls, decorated down to 1716 with precious hangings, were later adorned with paintings. On the walls on either side of the door are the four canvases by Tintoretto originally painted for the Sala delle Quattro Porte (*Mercury and the Graces; Minerva Driving Back Mars; Ariadne Found by Bacchus; Vulcan's Forge*): these works have been interpreted as an allegory of the wise government of the Venetian Republic or, with greater probability, the harmonious succession of the seasons, identified with the harmony of good government.

The latter explanation seems to be corroborated by the *putti* representing the seasons in the previous room, beside the original location of these paintings. On the wall opposite the window is the *Rape of Europa* by Paolo Veronese and the *Return of Jacob with his Family* by Jacopo da Ponte, known as Bassano.

Access to the following room is through a doorway with a marble group attributed to Alessandro Vittoria.

Sala dell'Anticollegio, view of the fireplace.

Jacopo Bassano, Return of Jacob with His Family. *Sala dell'Anticollegio.*

Jacopo Tintoretto, Peace, Grace and Minerva Banishing Mars. *Sala dell'Anticollegio.*

Sala del Collegio

The **Sala del Collegio** was
intended for assemblies of the
Magistratura, called the "Pien
Collegio," made up of the
Signoria (the Minor Consiglio),
the three *Capi della
Quarantia*, and the three
Zonte (the Savi del Consiglio,
Savi di Terraferma and Savi
degli Ordini). In this chamber
they received ambassadors,
and it was therefore necessary
for it to be particularly
splendid. In the mid-16th
century the decoration
consisted essentially of a
painting by Domenico Zorzi
depicting a Map of the
Venetian Dukedom, a large
clock and paintings, which
Sansovino describes as by
Giovanni Bellini and Titian,
without, unfortunately,
specifying their subjects.
Records also show that there
was another painting of the
*Doge Lorenzo before the Holy
Spirit* by Parrasio Micheli. The
room's structure, already fixed
in its main features soon after
1483, was completed with the
present decorations after the
fire of 1574, when it was
rapidly redecorated. Francesco
Bello and Andrea Faentin
made the wooden wainscoting
and carved ceiling (1576), to
designs by Palladio, who may
have collaborated with Rusconi
(1574–1575). The splendid

*Sala del Collegio, view
towards the throne.*

Paolo Veronese,
Venice Enthroned
with Justice and Peace.
Sala del Collegio, ceiling.

paintings on the ceiling were executed by Veronese in 1575, and we know that the work was complete on the death of Doge Venier (1578). The fact that the decoration was completed so swiftly certainly helped to confer on the chamber its distinctive unity of design. The wooden benches and dais are original and hence quite different from those in the other rooms, nearly always much later work. The dossals, however, are of a later date, replacing those destroyed in the fire of 1574. The very fine chimney-piece between the windows is by Gerolamo Campagna (1585–1595). The cycle of paintings on the ceiling is meant to extol the power and glory of Venice: the central compartments represent *Mars and Neptune, Faith the Strength of the Republic*, and *Venice Enthroned with Justice and Peace*, works that can be confidently ascribed to Veronese. At the sides are depicted the *Virtues*, each with its symbolic attribute. Above the dais is a painting that

represents *Sebastiano Venier Worshipping the Redeemer, with Saints*, also by Veronese. The walls are decorated with works by Tintoretto and his workshop (1581–1584): of particular interest is *Doge Andrea Gritti Worshipping the Virgin*, in which the master's hand seems evident.

Paolo Veronese, Faith the Strength of the Republic. *Sala del Collegio, ceiling.*

Sala del Senato

The **Sala del Senato** (or **Sala dei Pregadi**) was used for meetings of the senate, the most ancient institution in the Venetian state. We have, unfortunately, little information about the original decoration of the chamber, destroyed in the fire of 1574. Renovation of this room began some years later than in the case of the others, and was entrusted to Antonio da Ponte, under Doge Pasqual Cicogna, whose arms are carved among the decorations in the ceiling, the work of Cristoforo Sorte in the 1580s. Soon after the ceiling was finished, the paintings were added and were completed in 1595. The central panel, set within a carved and gilded surround, is the *Triumph of Venice*, painted by Jacopo and Domenico Tintoretto. Also noteworthy are the canvas of the *Dead Christ Supported by Angels*, by Tintoretto and assistants, on the walls above the dais, and on the opposite wall, the *Doges Lorenzo and Gerolamo Priuli Praying to the Virgin* by Palma il Giovane. On the wall opposite the windows are two large clocks, one of which bears the signs of the zodiac.

Jacopo Tintoretto and helpers, Dead Christ Supported by Angels, Adoration of Doges Pietro Lando and Marcantonio Trevisan with Their Patron Saints. *Sala del Senato.*

Tommaso Dolabella, Doge Pasquale Cicogna Adores the Eucharist, *ceiling. Sala del Senato.*

The **Sala del Senato** was also known as the "Sala dei Pregadi" because its members were invited ("pregati") in writing to attend council meetings. The term "senato" appeared in documents only at the end of the 14th century, when the

number of members was fixed at sixty. The *Serrata* (or "closure") of the Maggio Consiglio in 1297 severely pruned its powers, but the patricians, hostile to the idea of creating another political organ, restored to the Senate its original

political powers. The number of members increased rapidly in the 16th century by taking in the Quarantia, the Consiglio dei Dieci and a *Zonta* composed of sixty members, so that by the middle of the 16th century there were about 300 Senators. The Senate meetings were also attended by the Doge and his councillors as well as magistrates; it mainly dealt with political issues and also decided on declarations of war and extraordinary appointments.

View of the Sala del Senato.

*Jacopo Palma
il Giovane,* Venice
Receiving Gifts from
the Subject Provinces
Presented by Doge
Francesco Venier.
Sala del Senato.

*Jacopo Palma
il Giovane,* Doge Pietro
Loredan Beseeching
the Virgin for the End
of the Famine and
Victory Over the Turks.
Sala del Senato.

Sala del Consiglio dei Dieci

The **Sala del Consiglio dei Dieci** was restructured in 1533–1550 by Scarpagnino, and work at once began on the paintings, executed by Ponchino, the youthful Veronese and Zelotti. They first decorated the ceilings (1553–1554) with a cycle of illustrations probably devised by Daniele Barbaro and consisting largely of allegorical representations of the various functions of the councillors who met in this chamber. The ceiling has twenty-five compartments; the central one contains a 19th-century copy of the original work by Veronese, now in the Louvre. Among the finest paintings in this room are: the *Aged Oriental and a Young Woman* and *Juno Offering the Ducal Crown to Venice*, by Paolo Veronese, while the wall opposite the windows is adorned with a canvas by Aliense of the *Adoration of the Magi*. The painting of *Pope Alexander III Blessing Doge Ziani* was begun by Francesco Bassano but completed by assistants. The furnishings are at least in part original, but the seats of the members of the Council have been destroyed.

Paolo Veronese, Juno Offering the Ducal Crown to Venice. *Sala del Consiglio dei Dieci, ceiling.*

The **Consiglio dei Dieci** was a magistracy created in 1310 to deal with the Tiepolo-Querini conspiracy. It retained its emergency character for a long time, until in 1455 a decree of the Maggior Consiglio made it permanent. The Consiglio dei Dieci was empowered to investigate anyone who might threaten the security of the state. Its meetings were shrouded in mystery.

As its name implies, it consisted of ten ordinary members, appointed by the Senate and elected by the Maggior Consiglio, apart from the Doge himself. After the fall of the Republic, the Sala dei Dieci was turned into a baqueting hall, and then under Austrian rule into a court of law.

Antonio Vassillachi, called l'Aliense, Adoration of the Magi. *Sala del Consiglio dei Dieci.*

Sala del Consiglio dei Dieci, view.

Paolo Veronese,
Aged Oriental and
Young Woman.
*Sala del Consiglio
dei Dieci, ceiling.*

Sala della Bussola

The **Sala della Bussola**
served as a vestibule and
waiting-room for the previous
chamber; it was refurbished
and decorated in the mid-16th
century. Note the chimney-
piece, decorated by Jacopo
Sansovino and pupils. The
paintings, some attributed
to Paolo Veronese, represent
scenes from Venetian history.
In the **Armoury** are displayed
numerous suits of armour
for warfare or jousting, as
well as swords, halbards, and
cross-bows (almost two
thousand weapons all told).
Of special interest is the
Bust of Doge Morosini by
Filippo Parodi in the Sala
Morosini.

*Armour of Henri IV
of France. Armoury.*

Sala della Bussola.

*Armoury,
Sala Morosini.*

The **Sala della Bussola**
takes its name from a
wooden compass. Its
purpose was to mask the
passage on the left
leading to the secret
chamber where meetings
were held between the
Tre Capi and the
Inquisitors.

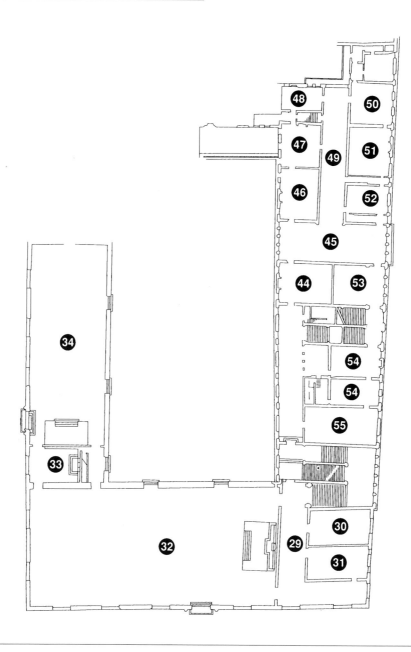

Liagò

Returning to the first floor
we come to the **Liagò**, the
chamber where nobles
gathered before and during
meetings of the Council.
It contains paintings by
Domenico Tintoretto, one
by Antonio Balestra, and one,
by Jacopo Palma il Giovane,
of *Doge Memmo Before the
Virgin with Patron Saints*
(dated 1615). The statues of
Adam and Eve, which used
to stand in the courtyard,
are by Antonio Rizzo.

Antonio Balestra,
Doge Giovanni Corner
Kneeling Before the
Virgin, *detail. Liagò.*

*Jacopo Palma
il Giovane,* Doge
Marcantonio Memmo
Before the Virgin with
Patron Saints. *Liagò.*

*View of the
Liagò.*

Sala della Quarantia Civil Vecchia

The **Sala della Quarantia Civil Vecchia** was the meeting-place for the forty members of the Quarantia Civile. This council, instituted in the 12th century, was divided in 1492 into two sections (Quarantia Vecchia and Quarantia Nuova), with different functions of the magistrature; in particular the Quarantia was responsible for passing sentence in serious criminal cases. The room's present appearance is due to a series of alterations in the course of the 17th century. On the walls are paintings by Pietro Malombra, *God the Father,* and *Venice Enthroned with the Virtues and Mercury Leading the Old and the Young Enchained,* a tabernacle with a 15th-century-panel of the *Madonna and Child,* and two canvases by Andrea Celesti depicting *Moses Destroying the Golden Calf* and *Moses Chastising the Jews for their Idolatry,* as well as a canvas representing *Venice among the Virtues Receiving the Sceptre of Power* by Giovan Battista Lorenzetti (1660); under the wooden dossals has been found an ancient fragment of painting in which the upper part of the Basilica of San Marco is still visible.

Quarantia Civil Vecchia, view.

Sala dell'Armamento

The **Sala dell'Armamento** (also known as the **Sala del Guariento**) was a store-room for weapons and munitions, and was originally connected to the Sala d'Armi and the Consiglio dei Dieci on the upper floors. At present it contains the remains of a fresco by Guariento, formerly in the Sala del Maggior Consiglio. Commissioned in about 1365, it represents the *Coronation of the Virgin*.

Badly damaged in the fire of 1577, it was then concealed behind the canvas of Tintoretto's *Paradise*; almost forgotten thereafter, it was only brought to light in the early years of the 20th century.

Guariento, fresco of the Coronation of the Virgin. *Sala dell'Armamento, or del Guariento.*

Sala del Maggior Consiglio

The **Sala del Maggior Consiglio** was the chamber where the most important legislative body of the Venetian state gathered to deliberate. The Maggior Consiglio or Grand Council was a very ancient body, comprising all noble Venetians above twenty years of age, whose mandate lasted one year (but they could stand for re-election). The assemblies were always presided over by the Doge and the Signoria. In 1297 the *Serrata* (or closure) of the Maggior Consiglio restricted the number of members and made them practically irremovable. Up to that time, the whole administration of the Venetian state had been effectively in the hands of the Maggior Consiglio; and even after it, when the legislative power had passed to the Senate, the Council still retained certain important prerogatives, such as the power to grant pardons. Its meetings were secret until the 16th century. The chamber was built in the mid-14th century, and the earliest paintings date from 1365. In that year Guariento, a Paduan artist, was commissioned to paint a fresco of the *Coronation of Maria* on the wall behind the throne. This fresco was badly

The **meetings of the Maggior Consiglio** were normally held on Sundays, and were preceded by the ringing of the bell of San Marco. The Signoria and the Dieci were responsible for ensuring that meetings were held behind closed doors and no weapons were brought into the chamber. The members, except for certain office-holders, would be seated in two rows, back-to-back. During the assemblies, armed guards were drawn up on both the Ponte della Paglia and in the Piazza, under the charge of the Procurators of San Marco, who waited under the loggia of the bell tower. It was in this chamber that the preliminary stages of the election of the Doge took place; voting would then be continued in the Sala dello Scrutinio. The election of a Doge was a particularly long and complicated procedure, in which voting alternated with the drawing of lots. A number of ballots,

damaged during the fire of 1577; it is now in the Sala del Guariento. In 1382 the Signoria urged the Procurators of San Marco to complete the decoration; towards the end of the 14th century they commissioned a number of painters to fresco the whole chamber; at the first sign of decay, these were replaced by paintings on canvas. It is likely, as Sansovino seems to suggest, that Guariento also painted other works that have not survived, and records show that the most celebrated painters of the day also worked in the chamber:

Gentile da Fabriano, Antonio Veneziano, Michelino da Besozzo, Alvise Vivarini, Jacobello del Fiore, Michele Giambono. The frescoes illustrated the history of relations between the Emperor and Pope, and the mediatory role of Venice, based on a set of inscriptions written by Petrarch during his stay in Venice (1362). It seems that these same inscriptions were also written on scrolls and displayed on the walls of the Grand Council hall. A document from 1425 not only cites the Petrarch texts, but comments on the imagery of the frescoes that accompanied

them, so it seems certain that they were finished by that date. In any case, we already know that under Doge Michele Steno (1400–1413) work was proceeding rapidly. There followed a period of stasis, due largely to the political and military difficulties of the Republic, and work was resumed only after 1470. It was decided not only to complete the gaps in the decoration, but also to renew the parts that had either decayed or failed to meet the changing taste of the day. The great fire of 1577 damaged both the wooden structures and the

corresponding to the number of nobles present, were placed in an urn; thirty of them were marked with the word "lector." Whoever received a ballot so marked remained in the chamber, the others left the room. The same

procedure was repeated to choose the electors, who in turn nominated forty "lectores"; then, by drawing lots, these were reduced to twelve, who elected twenty-five people and they, with a further ballot, were reduced to five. These

in turn had to elect forty-three people, reduced to eleven again by drawing lots. These eleven elected the forty-one electors of the Doge, who required a minimum of twenty-five votes to be elected.

Jacopo Tintoretto, Venice as Queen Offering an Olive Branch to Doge Nicolò da Ponte. *Sala del Maggior Consiglio, ceiling.*

View of the Sala del Maggior Consiglio.

*Paolo
Veronese,
The Triumph
of Venice.
Sala del Maggior
Consiglio, ceiling.*

Jacopo
Palma
il Giovane,
Venice Crowned
by Victory Triumphs
Over the Subject
Provinces.
Sala del Maggior
Consiglio, ceiling.

architecture of the Sala del Maggior Consiglio, while canvases and frescoes were almost completely destroyed. So extensive was the damage that the Signoria at first considered completely rebuilding the chamber. Finally partial reconstruction to a design by Antonio Rusconi was decided on; this retained the surviving features of the original, and the result is what one can see today. First it was decided to decorate the ceiling (by Cristoforo Sorte, 1582), and in 1587 a monk, Gerolamo Bardi, was commissioned to draft a detailed iconographic scheme, also based on the history of relations between Pope and Emperor, while adding episodes from the Fourth Crusade and other more strictly celebratory and symbolic themes. The central space was reserved for the glorification of the Republic. The design of the ceiling was conceived, in the taste of the period, as a sequence of large panels in which paintings on canvas were enclosed within sumptuous carved and gilded frames.There are three great paintings in the centre and twelve at the sides, while the spaces between the frames are filled with monochrome depictions of historical episodes or allegorical subjects. This imposing scheme was completed in the years of the dogeship of Nicolò da Ponte, and the most celebrated painters were, as usual, summoned to set their hands to the task. In 1579 Tintoretto and Veronese began work, followed by Jacopo Palma il Giovane and Francesco Bassano.The ceiling was completed by 1584, while the walls, begun in about 1590, were probably only completed early in the 17th century, except for Tintoretto's painting of *Paradise*, which took the artist from 1588 to 1594.

On the ceiling above the throne is Veronese's *Triumph of Venice*, a particularly rich

Tintoretto's painting of **Paradise** was originally executed on a smaller canvas for the Scuola Vecchia della Misericordia, and only later moved to the Sala del Maggior Consiglio, where it was finished in detail. A preparatory sketch for this splendid work is now in the Thyssen-Bornemisza Collection; it differs in some particulars from the finished painting.

Jacopo Tintoretto, Paradise, sketch for the painting in the Sala del Maggior Consiglio. Madrid, Thyssen-Bornemisza Collection. This sketch was entered in the competition of 1588 but did not win: the commission was only later assigned to Tintoretto after the death of Paolo Veronese, who had been originally chosen.

and spectacular work; while at the centre Jacopo Tintoretto (probably with assistants) depicted *Nicolò da Ponte Receiving the Laurel Crown from Venice* (1584). On the end wall is *Venice Crowned by Victory, which Receives the Subject Provinces*, by Jacopo Palma il Giovane: many preparatory studies for this work have been found. The twelve paintings at the sides of the ceiling (six per side) represent acts of heroism by the Republic's *condottieri* or episodes of war, such as the *Venetian Victory over the Milanese under Filippo Maria Visconti*, by Palma il Giovane, *Contarini's Conquest of Riva del Garda* by Tintoretto and assistants, and the *Battle of Maclodio* by Francesco Bassano. Immediately below the ceiling there runs a frieze with portraits of the first sixty-six doges, from Obelerio Antenoreo to Francesco Venier (1554–1556). Most of these portraits are imaginary; the commission was given to Jacopo Tintoretto but they were mostly painted by his son Domenico. Each doge holds a scroll on which are illustrated the most important achievements of his reign. Of all the paintings on the walls the most impressive is probably Tintoretto's *Paradise*, commissioned in 1588. In painting this vast

Jacopo Tintoretto,
Victory of the Venetians
Over the Ferrarese
at Argenta. *Sala
del Maggior Consiglio,
ceiling.*

canvas, Tintoretto was assisted by his son Domenico.The work is richly imaginative in composition and the sense of movement given to each of the figures. The paintings on the wall towards the inner courtyard were executed later, in the late 16th and early 17th centuries, and represent (as said above) Venice's mediation between Papacy and Empire. Between one episode and another are represented certain symbols of authority carried by the doges in public processions (though their origin does not lie in papal grants, as the iconographic scheme suggests, but rather dates back to Byzantine times). The sequence of the twelve episodes starts with the painting of *Alexander III in Venice with Doge Ziani* by C. and G. Caliari, near the dais. The other historical cycle, running along the wall towards the quay, depicts episodes from the Fourth Crusade, which was of great importance for Venice's subsequent commercial expansion in the East. Among the canvases of this cycle are *Army of the Crusaders Besieges Zara* by Andrea Vicentino, the *Surrender of Zara* and the *Conquest of Constantinople* by Domenico Tintoretto, the *Crusaders Besieging Constantinople* by Jacopo Palma il Giovane. On the wall opposite the dais, in the centre, is *Doge Contarini Returning to Venice in Triumph after Defeating the Genoese,* by Paolo Veronese and assistants, commemorating the victory of 1379.

Domenico Tintoretto, Portrait of Giovanni Mocenigo. *Sala del Maggior Consiglio, frieze.*

Domenico Tintoretto, Portrait of Mario Barbarigo. *Sala del Maggior Consiglio, frieze.*

A typical instance of *damnatio memoriae* can be seen in the frieze of the Doges of Venice. Doge Marin Faliero (1354-1355) was accused of conspiracy against the state and beheaded. In the panel where his portrait should appear there is a black curtain with this inscription: HIC EST LOCUS MARINI FALETHRI DECAPITATI PRO CRIMINIBUS (this is the place of Marin Faliero, beheaded for his crimes).

From the Sala della Quarantia Civil Nuova
to the Sala del Magistrato alle Leggi I

Next to the Sala del Maggior Consiglio is the **Sala della Quarantia Civil Nuova**, the council chamber for the magistrature instituted in 1492, which dealt with cases in the provinces subject to Venice. The chamber, restructured after 1577, contains paintings alluding to the functions of the magistracy, by artists of the early 17th century. The **Sala dello Scrutinio**, also restored in 1579–1599 after being damaged by fire, was where

Sala della Quarantia Civil Nuova, view.

Andrea Vicentino, The Battle of Lepanto. *Sala dello Scrutinio.*

Antonio Vassillachi, Clemency. *Sala dello Scrutinio, ceiling.*

and assistants; the others, which continue the series down to Doge Ludovico Manin (1789–1797) were the work of artists contemporary with the doges themselves. On the wall behind the dais is the very fine *Last Judgment* by Palma il Giovane (1594–1595: note the arms of Doge Francesco Foscari), which replaced Tintoretto's painting of the same subject, lost in the fire. On the end wall, towards the Scala Foscari, is the monument to Francesco Morosini (c. 1694) designed by A. Gaspari, with paintings by Lazzarini representing the achievements of this Venetian *condottiero*. The **Sala della Quarantia Criminal** is decorated with 17th-century stalls, while the walls of the **Sala del Magistrato alle Leggi I** display paintings by Flemish artists: *Paradise*, the *Fall of the Damned, Empyrean, Inferno*, the *Triptych of the Hermits* and the *Triptych of the Martyrdom of St. Liberata* by Hieronymus Bosch, and *Christ Mocked* by Quentin Metsys.

voting took place for elections to the various offices of state. A previous ceiling dated from the 1630s and was the work of Serlio, with paintings by Pordenone; the present one is by Sorte, with a series of carved and gilded mouldings. The scheme of decoration, devised by the monk Gerolamo de' Bardi, envisaged thirty-nine painted panels depicting naval victories by the Venetians in the East and the conquest of Padua. Nearly all the paintings were commissioned from Tintoretto and Veronese and their pupils. Changes were made to the program, so that some paintings were added in the following century. The frieze repeats the motif of the portraits of doges (as in the Sala del Maggior Consiglio): the earliest were by Tintoretto

Hieronymus Bosch,
Paradise and Empyrean.
*Sala del Magistrato
alle Leggi I.*

Hieronymus Bosch,
Triptych of the Hermits,
*detail. Sala del
Magistrato alle Leggi I.*

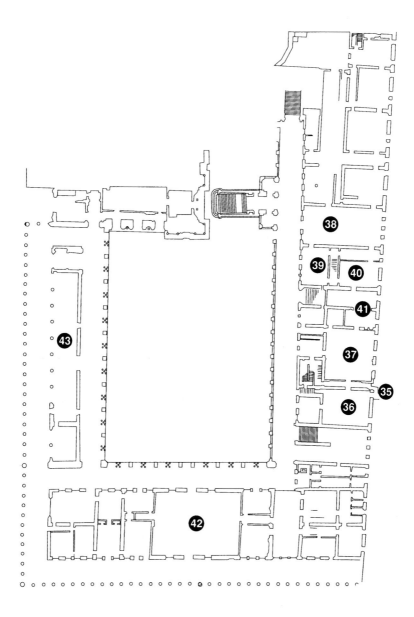

Plan of the loggias.
35. Bridge of Sighs
36. Sala dei Censori
37. Sala dell'Avogadria
38. Cancelleria Inferiore
39. Sala della Bolla
40. Sala della Milizia da Mar
41. Sala dello Scrigno
42. Sala del Piovega
43. Loggia Foscara

Bridge of Sighs

A corridor leads on to the celebrated **Bridge of Sighs**, initially designed by Rusconi, continued by Da Ponte and completed by Antonio and Tommaso Contino (1614). The bridge was built to join the Doge's Palace with the newly-built **Prigioni Nuove** alongside. It is closed and roofed over: the decoration of the exterior foreshadows the Baroque style and it is decorated with bas-reliefs of *Justice* and the arms of the Doge Marino Grimani (1595–1606). The name is a 19th century literary invention. The Prigioni Nuove were designed by Da Ponte but constructed by Antonio Contin, who completed them in the early 17th century.

The Bridge of Sighs.

From the Sala dei Censori to the Sala della Bolla

Returning to the Doge's Palace, we enter the **Sala dei Censori**, where a frieze presents the portraits of magistrates by Domenico Tintoretto.

The **Sala dell'Avogadria** was the council chamber for a very ancient magistracy, made up of three members (or *"Avogadri"*) elected by the Maggior Consiglio; it dealt with fiscal problems and acted as public prosecutor in trials, with the principal task of ensuring application of the laws. On the wall by the entrance is a *Resurrection with Three Avogadri* by Domenico Tintoretto and the *Madonna in Glory with Three Avogadri* by Leandro Bassano. Other paintings by D. Tintoretto are on the wall opposite the windows.

In the **Sala dello Scrigno** there is an 18th-century cabinet containing the *Libro d'Oro*, in which all the nobility were enrolled, and the *Libro d'Argento*, which listed the citizenry. The walls are decorated with portraits of Avogadri and Censors, notable among which are the *Portrait of Three Avogadori* by Pietro Uberti and the *Virgin in Glory and Child with Three Avogadri* by Nicolà Renieri. The **Sala della Milizia da Mar**, housed the meeting place for the *Zonta* whose task was to keep the galleys fitted out and properly manned, contains original Cinquecento furnishings and paintings by the school of Tiepolo.

The **Sala della Bolla** was the chamber of the official who approved official transactions; it, too, is decorated with portraits of Avogadri and Censors.

Domenico Tintoretto, Annunciation and Portraits of Three Avogadri. *Sala dei Censori.*

View of the Sala dei Censori.

Domenico Tintoretto,
Resurrection and
Three Avogadri.
Sala dell'Avogadria.

Pietro Uberti, Portraits
of Three Avogadri.
Sala dello Scrigno.

Cortile dei Senatori, Porticato and Arco Foscari, Scala dei Giganti

Passing through the loggia, we descend to the floor below and emerge into the **Cortile dei Senatori**, probably a gathering place for senators before the assemblies began. The façade was built in the early 16th century and is attributed to Giorgio Spavento; in imitation of Rizzo's design for the façade alongside; the upper storey is lightened by a row of windows with columns and tympana, decorated in polychrome marble. Opposite stands the **Porticato Foscari** (1440–1450) which, in ancient times—even before the year 1000—was the only fortified entrance to the castle. At the head of the portico, on the opposite side the Porta della Carta, is the **Arco Foscari**, begun in the 1460s, still with a Gothic flavour but with Renaissance ornaments. At the top are a series of pinnacles with statues of *St. Mark and the Liberal Arts* by Bregno and Rizzo. The **Sala dei Giganti** was designed by Antonio Rizzo in 1483-1485, and the sculptures were completed by 1491. The name comes from the two stone statues of *Mars* and *Neptune* carved by Jacopo Sansovino and set on the upper parapet in 1567. The structure is dressed with marble and decorated with bas-reliefs in full Renaissance style.

Some rooms of the Doge's Palace can be seen only by guided parties, called "segret itineraries." It is possible to visit the offices and Sala della Cancelleria, which used to contain the most reserved documents, the secret passage leading to the Sala del Consiglio dei Dieci, the Sala dei Tre Capi and the Sala degli Inquisitori, whose ceiling is decorated with canvases by Tintoretto (c. 1556) depicting the *Return of the Prodigal Son Surrounded by Four Virtues.* Other rooms that can be visited are the Torture Chamber, the prisons under the leads, known as "I Piombi," where Giacomo Casanova was imprisoned, and the kitchens of the palace in the depths of the building.

Scala dei Giganti, detail of the reliefs on the sides of the staircase.

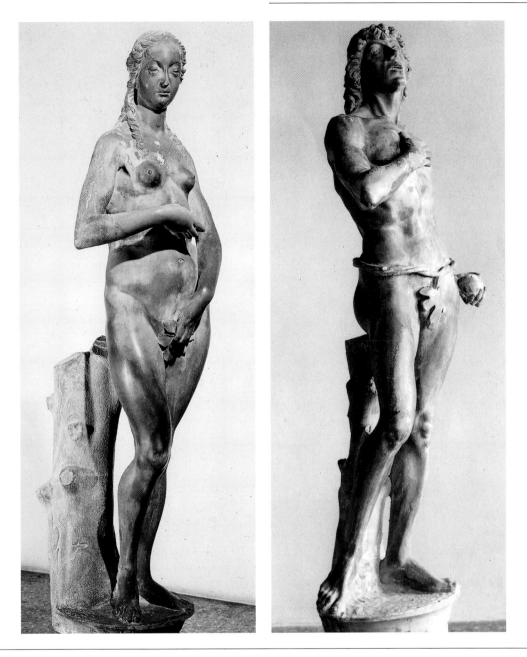

Antonio Rizzo,
of Adam and Eve. Liagò.
The statues were
originally installed
in the niches of the Arco
Foscari, but today they
have been substituted
by bronze copies.

The Scala de i Giganti.

Jacopo Sansovino,
Mars and Neptune.
Scala dei Giganti.

Photograph Credits
Graziano Arici, Venice
Cameraphoto, Venice
Electa Archive/Sergio Anelli, Milan
Museo Correr Photograph Archive, Venice

This volume was printed by Elemond S.p.a.
at the plant in Martellago (Venice)